To Al Beck,
a wonderful teacher,
mentor, and friend
who helped me unleash
my inner penguin
many years ago.

Special thanks to Paul Erickson,
formerly of the New England Aquarium,
who graciously shared his knowledge
of these fascinating little creatures.

Copyright © 2007 by Bob Barner.
All rights reserved.

Book design by Sara Gillingham and Katie Jennings.
Typeset in Softie.
The illustrations in this book were rendered in cut and torn paper.
Manufactured in China.

Library of Congress Cataloging-in-Publication Data
Barner, Bob.
Penguins, penguins, everywhere! / by Bob Barner.
p. cm.
ISBN-13: 978-0-8118-5664-5
ISBN-10: 0-8118-5664-X
1. Penguins—Juvenile literature. I. Title.
QL696.S473B367 2007
598.47—dc22
2006020960

Distributed in Canada by Raincoast Books
9050 Shaughnessy Street, Vancouver, British Columbia V6P 6E5

10  9  8  7  6  5  4  3  2  1

Chronicle Books LLC
680 Second Street, San Francisco, California 94107

www.chroniclekids.com

# Penguins, Penguins, Everywhere!

### By Bob Barner

chronicle books · san francisco

Some penguins live in icy places.

and some live in the heat.

Their colors help them hide

when they fish for fishy treats.

Cold penguins huddle close

with penguin heat to share.

DaddieS warm fragile eggs

with tender, special care.

Hot penguins fluff their feathers

co cool off from the sun.

Their chicks call out from shady

caves to ask for food and fun.

Noisy penguins waddle

and toboggan to the sea.

Each one honks to find

its mate wherever it may be.

Penguins watch for sneaky seals

as they swim and splash and play.

Sleepy little penguins end

another perfect day.

# Penguin **?** Puzzler

Lizards

Octopuses

Sharks

## What do penguins eat?

Krill

Squid

Fish

## What do penguins say?

Honk Honk

Yak Yak

Hee Haw Hee Haw

penguins?

Seals

Snakes

Orcas

Gulls

Dive

**Why do penguins look the way they do?**

Tiptoe

Waddle

**How do penguins move?**

In the water, black feathers blend in with the ocean bottom. This makes it hard for hungry penguin eaters to see the penguins from above.

White feathers blend in with the light colored sky so hungry penguin eaters can't spot penguins from below.

# Penguin Parade

## Emperor
### Antarctica

45 inches
(114 cm)

90 pounds
(41 kg)

## Chinstrap
### South Sandwich Islands

24 inches
(61 cm)

10 pounds
(4 1/2 kg)

## Fiordland
### New Zealand

23 inches
(58 cm)

6 1/2 pounds
(3 kg)

## Erect-Crested
### Islands off the coast
### of New Zealand

20 inches
(51 cm)

8 pounds
(3 1/2 kg)

## Black-Footed
### Also called "African Penguin"
### Africa

20 inches
(51 cm)

6 1/2 pounds
(3 kg)

22 inches
(56 cm)

13 pounds
(6 kg)

## Gentoo
### Falkland Islands

## Magellanic
### Argentina

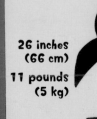

26 inches
(66 cm)

11 pounds
(5 kg)

## Yellow-Eyed
### New Zealand

30 inches (76 cm)

11 pounds (5 kg)

# King
## South Georgia Island

28 inches
(71 cm)

30 pounds
(14 kg)

# Humboldt
## Peru

25 inches
(64 cm)

9 pounds
(4 kg)

# Macaroni
## Falkland Islands

28 inches
(71 cm)

9 1/2 pounds
(4 1/2 kg)

# Galápagos
## Galápagos Islands

20 inches
(51 cm)

5 pounds
(2 1/4 kg)

# Snares Island
## Snares Island

16 inches
(41 cm)

6 1/2 pounds
(3 kg)

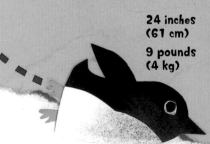

# Royal
## Macquarie Island

27 inches
(69 cm)

10 pounds
(4 1/2 kg)

# Rockhopper
## South America

16 inches (41 cm)

5 pounds (2 1/4 kg)

# Adélie
## Antarctica

24 inches
(61 cm)

9 pounds
(4 kg)

# Little Blue
## also called "Fairy Penguin"
## New Zealand

16 inches
(41 cm)

2 1/2 pounds
(1 kg)